Finding Grace

Kerrie Woodhouse

FINDING GRACE

Copyright © **2016 Kerrie Woodhouse**

All rights reserved.

Melbourne, Vic, Australia

No parts of this publication may be reproduced, stored in a retrieval system, or transmitted in any form or by any means, electronic, mechanical, photocopying, recording, or otherwise, without the prior written permission of the copyright owner.

This book is sold subject to the condition that it shall not, by way of trade or otherwise, be lent, resold, hired out, or otherwise circulated without the publisher's prior consent in any form of binding or cover other than that in which it is published and without a similar condition including this condition being imposed on the subsequent purchaser. Under no circumstances may any part of this book be reproduced for resale.

To Isabelle:

For showing me what grace looks like.

This book is dedicated to someone I cared about very much.

Download a free printable card today to send to someone you care about.

Go on. Make their day.

http://tiny.cc/gracecard

Download your free card at:
http://tiny.cc/gracecard

Contents

Introduction 8

What is this thing called grace? 12

The origin of the 'Grace Girls' 74

Introduction

This book is dedicated to my very dear friend who was bravely battling breast cancer at around the time I started drawing these little girls. At such times, we take comfort wherever we can find it and somehow these big-eyed girls offered me just that.

They gave me the chance to escape the world, even for a short time. They seemed to understand, could be whatever I needed: a joyful celebration of life, an expression of sorrow, a calm, reflective companion.

What mattered is that they were always there, trusting me to find the strength to support my friend through a difficult time and helping me find the grace to let her go.

I count myself so lucky to have engaged in a creative process that took on a life of its own. Through the process of creating a quick daily drawing I found myself contemplating grace and what it means to me.

This book is the result of all that contemplation: a mix of my own thoughts, words of others that resonated with me and, of course, the big-eyed girls that kept me company.

Come with me on that journey.

What is this thing called grace?

It seems to be something we understand better than we articulate. We use it and hear it in many different contexts, probably without giving it much thought.

But if you do give some thought to its many facets you will discover it to be mysterious, perhaps even magical. Grace is an important concept for which we must each find our own personal meaning.

Finding grace is finding a life of greater ease. It is a way of living in full appreciation of all that is wonderful, while finding acceptance of that which we cannot change. Grace is that magical quality that - if we can find it - smooths our path through life.

"I do not at all understand the mystery of grace - only that it meets us where we are but does not leave us where it found us."

Anne Lamott

The first image the word grace conjures in my mind is that of the ballerina - for me, she is the epitome of grace.

Grace is beauty and elegance in many things. The dancer shows us beauty and grace in movement. We watch her poise and refined movements and wonder if it is possible for us to move through life with her ease and finesse.

Her dance is not easy, although she makes it seem so. Her dance requires strength and discipline but in spite of this, she does not lose sight of its joy or fail to express its beauty.

She is supple enough to accommodate the challenges.

She is grace.

"As in nature, as in art, so in grace; it is rough treatment that gives souls, as well as stones, their luster."

Thomas Guthrie

There is also beauty and elegance in form, even in stillness. What is the delicate arch of the orchid stem and its tender bloom, if not graceful? Grace is ever present in nature, if we care to look.

"Everything that slows us down and forces patience, everything that sets us back into the slow circles of nature, is a help. Gardening is an instrument of grace."

May Sarton

Grace in action makes things better than they were before. To grace a thing is to add beauty and elegance. Flowers grace a room. Grace notes embellish melodies.

What graces your world today?

Grace is not merely something to be passively observed, it is the active enhancement of our world and experience. Grace in action is honouring, favouring and lending dignity.

"The ideal man bears the accidents of life with dignity and grace, making the best of circumstances."

Aristotle

"A high station in life is earned by the gallantry with which appalling experiences are survived with grace."

Tennessee Williams

For all its dignity and propriety, grace is still humble.

"Grace is having a commitment to - or an acceptance of - being ineffective and foolish"

Anne Lamott

Those that behave with good grace are willing, cheerful and ungrudging. Grace is a worthy attribute. It speaks of forgiveness and mercy, of decency and propriety. It is perhaps something we continually work for. It describes the sort of higher spiritual values that we would want to demonstrate in our time on the earth.

"Learn to… be what you are, and learn to resign with a good grace all that you are not."

Henri Frederic Amiel

"Grace must find its expression in life otherwise its not grace."
Karl Barth

If we can find grace, it leaves its mark upon us. A life well lived with grace lights the face. Beauty from within will always shine through.

"The rose that grows in grace will blossom into beauty."

Nancy B Brewer

"When grace is joined with wrinkles, it is adorable. There is an unspeakable dawn in happy old age."

Victor Hugo

"No spring nor summer beauty hath such grace as I have seen in one autumnal face."
John Donne

Grace holds significant meaning for those of a Christian faith. Grace can mean divine assistance, the free unmerited favour of God towards man.

Regardless of religion, the reference to grace as a prayer is likely to have some meaning for us all. That grace is thankfulness, a blessing, a benediction. That grace is gratitude.

What are you grateful for?

"There is a loveliness to life that does not fade. Even in the terrors of the night, there is a tendency toward grace that does not fail us."

Robert Goolrich

"Happiness is the experience of living every moment with love, grace and gratitude"

Denis Waitley

For all its complexity and layers of meaning grace is such a simple word.

For me the word itself conveys so much of its meaning. It is a short word - just a single syllable, for grace is humble not flamboyant. It is in its simplicity that its elegance lies.

"Beauty of style and harmony and grace and good rhythm depend on simplicity."
Plato

Even the sound of the word tells so much. The hard *g* sound at the start reminds us that grace requires strength. But with the soft *s* sound we remember that this is not the strength of brute force, but the gentle strength to nurture, to forgive, and to rise above the petty minutiae of daily life.

This, to me, is the pivotal element of grace: it represents spiritual wisdom. Something we gain through experience, that brings peace to ourselves as well as others.

To have grace is to have the spiritual wisdom to be kind, generous and forgiving. Grace is the spiritual wisdom to express appreciation for the beautiful world around us and, in so doing, to be part of that beauty.

"Grace is not part of consciousness; it is the amount of light in our souls, not knowledge nor reason."

Pope Francis

The Origin of the 'Grace Girls'

The 'Grace girls' were born of a challenge called the 100 Day Project, which was created by Elle Luna. The challenge involved coming up with a creative project that you could do daily for 100 consecutive days and post each day's output on Instagram. "Show up, show up, show up and eventually the muse shows up too."

I had just started drawing little 'warm up' girls in a small square journal. I had limited my supplies to a set of travel watercolours, a waterproof pen, a grease pencil and a white marker. The idea was to draw a quick character in ten minutes or so. The time constraint liberated me from perfection. The supplies constraint removed the dilemma of choice of media. Subject matter was predetermined. Excuses eliminated. Just draw. It seemed to be a perfect exercise for the 100 Day Project.

I usually always begin by making the irises with my finger. The eyes are my favourite thing to draw and I always felt I needed to see her eyes to know what the rest of her face would be like and what she might want to wear. There is a curiously intimate connection created by making her eyes with my fingerprint. I think it makes her an extension of me, or at least a part of me. Once the iris is in I draw the rest of the face, hair and body with either my waterproof ink pen or my grease pencil. The grease pencil if I feel like I need a bit of a return to childhood. It feels like you are drawing with a stubby wax crayon. The ink pen gives a more refined look, best if I feel calm before I begin.

Then it is time to add more colour. I limit the palette to about three colours most often. Partly to reduce the time wasting burden of choice, and partly because it gives a harmonised drawing. I will already have chosen one colour for her eyes so that leaves me with only one or two more decisions to make. Sometimes I add patterns or motifs in the background while I am thinking. The aim is to keep the hand moving and not stop and think too much.

The final touch is to add the highlights to the eyes with the white pen. Now she comes to life.

It occurred to me that the girls are always very childlike, both in design and execution, but they seem to have very adult eyes. They seem to be very wise. They blend the benefits of experience with the sense of awe that is the natural privilege of childhood. For me, that is grace.

While I was participating in the 100 day challenge I was also fortunate enough to be spending considerable time with Isabelle, who was bravely battling breast cancer. We would draw together and talk a lot. Grace was something we discussed quite often. I am sure it is because of these conversations that one day 'Grace' who is now on the cover of this book, appeared in my sketchbook.

Every day I drew a girl and found myself thinking about grace. Mystical, magical grace. Eventually I decided to try and organise these thoughts by putting them in a book. And that is how the book you now hold in your hands came to be.

Unfortunately I did not manage to finish this book in time for my dear friend to see it. But I do feel her gentle grace when I look at my Grace girls. I hope you do too.

Thank you for sharing my journey towards finding grace.

If you would like to see the creative process for yourself please go to http://tiny.cc/graceprocess to access a free video I've made as a token of my gratitude to you for joining me along the way.

www.ingramcontent.com/pod-product-compliance
Lightning Source LLC
Chambersburg PA
CBHW042228010526
44113CB00045B/2859